Enigmatic

Daragh Fleming

For all the people who spend too much time on the internet.
(and for my mother, naturally.)

"Now I am quietly waiting for the catastrophe of my personality to seem beautiful again, and interesting, and modern."

– Frank O'Hara

Praise for Enigmatic by Daragh Fleming

Heartfelt, lyrical, and moving, Daragh Fleming's poems in Enigmatic steer the reader through an exploration of a young man navigating a world that leaves him all-too-frequently isolated; for, despite living in an era of supposed connectivity, these touching, open, fresh, and honest poems show us a world often lacking in true connection, a lack the poet strives to see filled. Loneliness, longing for another, for love, for companionship at least, these poems demonstrate the power of words to comfort and offer consolation. Full of striking, potent, and vivid images, expressing genuine emotional and mental pain and loss, the poems contain flashes of a dark, brittle, and truthful humour. Self-revealing to an excoriating degree, they demonstrate a powerful way with words and language, and echo with love, that yearning for connection with another, and that equally strong urge to console.
– Arnold Thomas Fanning.

"A collection of poetry that finds itself dancing in-between life's most profound moments, Enigmatic by Daragh Fleming explores all of our unsaid everythings. From the stark to the absurd, to the humorous and the deeply melancholic, it is startling the skill with which the author deals with such delicate complexity. The result is a series of poetics that uses a beautiful simplicity of communication, one that makes this book accessible, a delight to consume, and yet immediately takes the reader to a place of knowing, of memory, even if that feeling is remembered as something glanced from the corner of one's eye. Enigmatic is the complex everyday distilled into a shared understanding, something that helps us all as we try to find our way home." – Stuart McPherson, End Ceremonies (Broken Sleep Books 2023)

Through a window unable to shut properly, we find an open, earnest and honest new collection from Daragh Fleming, a refreshingly truthful take on growing up between the darkness and the light, under the glare of social media and the disconnect of a right swipe on Tinder. Enigmatic examines that disconnect, the roundabout ways we've been programmed to connect; the swipes, the likes, the tweets in place of direct conversation or confession – I wanted to call and tell you that you're lovely, but we don't do things like that... So I liked something you posted on the internet. These are modern lines penned from the outside while contemplating if the inside is any warmer. As the growing Lonely Boy himself says – the size of the darkness and light is something we control and it's fascinating to watch Fleming begin to master this very control. In a world that needs its Marvel superheroes, Daragh splashes an F across his t-shirt for a fragility that is fearless. – Damien B Donnelly, Poet and Podcast Producer

"As with "Lonely Boy", Daragh Fleming shows his depth of perception in "Enigmatic". These are poems of stillness, searching and quiet contemplation. Always honest, Fleming returns and returns again to the great act of understanding and excavating the self." – Luke Morgan

"This book is not academic enough to endorse." – A Creative Writing professor with more than two decades of academic experience.

Contents

Foreword

"Enigmatic" is a collection of poetry that captures the essence of the human experience in all its intricacies and complexities. Written by the talented poet Daragh Fleming, these poems offer a glimpse into the depths of the human heart and mind, inviting readers to explore the mysteries and contradictions that make us who we are.

Through his words, Fleming explores themes of love and loss, pain and healing, joy and sorrow, all the while maintaining a sense of enigma and mystery that keeps readers engaged and intrigued. His mastery of language and imagery allows readers to see the world through his eyes, to experience the world in a new and profound way.

Each poem in this collection is a carefully crafted work of art, a testament to Fleming's dedication to his craft and his willingness to explore the depths of the human soul. His words speak to the universal human experience, reminding us that we are all connected by the same hopes, fears, and dreams.

From the haunting beauty of "Transcription" to the bittersweet nostalgia of "Grey Tracksuit," each poem in Enigmatic invites the reader to delve deeper into their own emotions and experiences. With a keen eye for detail and a gift for language, Daragh Fleming captures the fleeting moments that shape our lives and the indescribable emotions that accompany them.

As the reader turns the pages of "Enigmatic," they will find themselves drawn into a world of beauty and wonder, a world that is at once familiar and yet wholly new. This collection is a testament to the power of poetry, to its ability to capture the essence of the human experience and to move us in ways that are both profound and enduring.

I am honoured to have had the privilege of editing this collection, and I am confident that readers will find in these pages a source of inspiration, solace, and joy.

Rebecca Rijsdijk, Editor-in-Chief Sunday Mornings at the River, 2023

Prayer Before We Begin

I'm writing this now to remember this feeling,
of being on the cusp,
caught between worlds,
old life fading,
no longer welcome to return.

New life expanding,
like the light of the torch before me,
as I walk Lexi on the same
country roads, all green and obvious.
I've walked dogs here
for two decades or more.

This is it now.
This is it now.

No going back,
nothing will be the same.
Are you ready for this,
as the clouds break apart
and acknowledge me with rain?

Things I Need To Tell You

There is so much to say.
Too much to say now.
Too urgent to say later.

On How Language Creates Our Reality

If you spell 'live' backwards
it spells 'evil'.
And if you spell death backwards
it spells 'htaed' which is nonsense.

So if living is evil
and death makes no sense
then perhaps you and I should
clamber through the universe
before this nonsense tries to kill us
and before the mobs sends us to Hell
for simply trying to live.

Ancestral

I am alive but not in the traditional sense.
Creeping inside floorboards, the icy grip of October.
Steeped in millennia, a thick soup of fated cosmos.
Purged and reborn from the hearts of exploding diamond
suns.

I am alive forever but never now.
The potential, that which makes all but is nothing
flowing inside the blood coursing through veins.
The names of a thousand generations forgotten until remembered

I am alive in all the ways you are not.
I am the life you become in death.
The amalgamation of eternity is us.
We are most alive when we no longer exist.

The entire world, past and future becomes I.
The most alive in all the ways you will never understand.

Daragh Fleming

Heartache in Between

They shake my hand like men trying
to sway my vote and I smile
and hope for a bathroom to escape to.
In a coffee shop on a Wednesday
you triumphantly tell me that you've
never read anything I've written.
A dissolvable Vitamin C drink spills
and spreads into cream carpet
as another woman sends another text
to cancel a date last minute
and I sit here as the carpet stains
wondering what this is all about,
what exactly is the purpose of all of this?

Double Exposure

Nothing makes sense until I am here again
at the frayed edges of non-reality.
Threads are pulled and seams uncreated
as I forget an entire world in exchange.

The blurry remnants of another dimension,
kaleidoscope chaos running circles in my soul.
It is now impossible to know which one is real;
The difference beneath or the dullness above.

I drift and shift   between   worlds
unable to remember one
whilst I exist in the other.
Only at the brittle borders do I recall.

Crossing the threshold, I remember both at once
like photographs that have been doubly exposed.

To The God(s) Departed

Briefly, I leave this Earth to search
for a God who might have answers.
The many Gods historically assigned to our planet
are uninterested, or perhaps just unaware.

I spend my spare minutes between meetings looking
for a God more hands-on.
One who might speak louder than a thundering
waterfall
or more clearly than the white noise of torrential rain.

Unholy, I climb the carcasses of old stars
sounding out the shape of an improvement.
only to return in time for dinner.
No new Gods found, no evidence of our quiet God's
existence.

Wednesday Alone

A man with salesman's eyes stopped by
today to ask about the van. "It's not for sale"
says I beneath a warm and cloudy sky. The
first words I'd spoken all day. Later, a woman
named Marika with tattoos all over dropped
off a package. Again I tried to talk but she
was in a rush. I must have looked half-mad
in the garden anyway, greeting her between
flowers and vehicles that weren't for sale. The
only other words I spoke that afternoon were
to Lexi and myself. Telling her that she was the best
girl as her tail wagged, telling myself that tomorrow
would be better, hoping I was right, knowing there
was no guarantee.

Note to You

I've been reluctant lately
to write for fear that I have
nothing to say and then
I remembered that part
of my job is to make people
feel less alone and how
common this fear is. So
I wrote this for you if
you're reluctant to write
for fear of having nothing
to say – you are not alone.

Down and Across

Just in case,
Because I know that
Life
Has its ups and downs
No matter what time of the day
Meaning – day or night – it
Doesn't matter to me, I
Mean it
Yours
Is a call I will always take even if it's
Meaningless or serious or somewhere in between

I Struggled To Forget

Restless like anxious knees
bouncing beneath tables.
The type of thing only those
who have anxious knees understand.

I tell myself that if I do something
productive I'll feel better
and this is sometimes true but often
it just adds to an ever-growing list
of things I need to finish.

I do not wave at magpies.

But I do mentally acknowledge their presence.
So I guess you could say I'm a little bit -stitious.

I used to have a recurring nightmare of the apoca-
lypse
but the dreams stopped
which makes me think that the world
has already ended
and that the dream was just a memory
I struggled to forget.

Anyone who claims to understand Nietzsche is a liar
and no one goes through anything alone
despite how it might feel.

I Wish

I wish I could tell you that I won a fiver
on a scratch card last Tuesday
and about how long it took me to get out
of Dublin on Friday night.

I wish I could complain to you about how
expensive hotels are these days
or tell you about how hungover I am
and how I am never drinking again.

I wish I could send you videos you'd find funny
and tell you about the girl who shifted me last
Saturday and about the girl I didn't have the balls
to talk to in the end.

I wish I could waste entire Sundays talking shite
and pretend to understand what you do for a living.
I wish I could meet you for a coffee on a Thursday
afternoon
just because.

I wish I could send you drafts of the stories I write
and celebrate your wins with you and buy
bottles of whiskey that you'll never drink
when it's your birthday.

I wish I could reminisce about the good old days
when all we worried about was chasing women
and whether basketball training would be overly
difficult and whether we'd have enough money for
chips.

I wish I could meet your family
and be there at your wedding.

I wish I could have been the world's best uncle
to children who have your laugh.

I wish a thousand things.
I wish things could have been different.
I wish you could have told me of the pain.
But above all else I just wish you could be here...

Second Edition

How can I explain it to you?
How can I convey what it is like
to be outside of something you
have always been within so naturally?

I am a window unable to close properly
leaving a draught to swirl around the room.
I am the wobble in a table's legs,
the creak of an old door.

I am the misprint, the typo, the
smudged ink on wet paper.
I am the unexpected second child,
the after-thought again and again.

Not of design, but of circumstance,
the piece that does not belong.
The shoes that will never fit.
You are of life; I am outside of it

New Voicemail

i know that spending this much time alone is danger-
ous
bandages made from whiskey and nicotine cannot

stop the bleeding. ignoring another phone call now
leave it go to voicemail. maybe she has a better expla-
nation

it is not that I want to be alone but rather
i do not know how to be myself without it

have you ever spent an entire day without speaking?
i have. hundreds of times. it feels

like me in the most chilling way. like leaving
a voicemail for someone who is already dead.

Kaleidoscope

Before we began there were darkness and light
and the end was always clear.
Tendons grew like saplings first,
hearts began to beat like the wings of eagle nestlings.
Eyes enlarged and opened without sight.

And then we began.

The light grew and shrunk.
The darkness followed suit.
A kaleidoscope of life, spiralling
in an infinite cacophony of cosmic possibility.

And still, the end was always clear

Some of us catch on early
and some of us never at all
that the size of the darkness and the light
is something we control.
It is our hand that turns the kaleidoscope.

Fault

When I am angry, and angry toward you
I am not angry *with* you.
This distinction is imperative.

When foul moods find me,
and they do so often,
this is not your fault
even when I make you feel that it is.

When I say I don't care,
I don't mean
I don't care about you.

I mean I don't care about me
and you are the misfortunate mirror.

When the sun droops and fades, and the rain
splat-splat-splats
it is not your fault
that I have forgotten my raincoat.
When darkness comes and I
struggle to find my way,
it is not you who has hidden it.

None of it has been your fault
but I have often made it your problem.
And all of this is to say that

I do love you.

Which I don't say as often as you deserve
but which I do really feel
with every day that comes.

This Storm

You think that me spending this
time alone means I somehow love
you less. But the opposite
is true.

I am isolating now exactly because I
love you. If we were to sail together
now I would likely
sink you.

With cutting words
and moodiness
that sting as sore as day
old sunburn.

I do not wish to torment you
when the storm is already raging
and you alone amongst the waves;
I will veer this storm from near you.

Damp Skull

You know surely by now,
having involuntarily dwelled
inside your own damp skull
for so long, with the thorns
and daisies and nettles
and the bitter unripe berries,

You must know now at least
as you fail to fall asleep
with the thump-thump
of your heart against sheets.

You have to certainly know
that you
in your puzzling way
think far too much, and far too often.

This Is All Quite New

I used to not feel this way. Genuinely.
When I was much younger it did not exist
So when it crept in all Biblical, I didn't notice.

Irritable.

                                               Every-

thing anyone says

                                                     is annoy-

ing.
          Jumping from one thought to the next.
                    The incessant checking of
phones
                   and emails.
Tired eyes   and   strained
skin.

The back aches

Neck aches

Sore teeth

Tense jaw.
                 Closed throat.
                    The feeling of falling
behind.
Of failure,
of not being good enough

The anger. So much anger.
                                        The
anxious flickers.
          The sweat-ful sleep.
          The reluctance to begin the day.

The disdain for being social.
        The lack of joy and the frustration
due to this lack of joy.

The relentless

unyielding

pressure.
And
        The absolute refusal to talk about any of it.

Up From The Darkness

Discolouration flees as freckles
flood faces with sunshine's adoration.
That harsh bite of winter withers;
A fading happily-forgotten memory.
Bare thighs and calves and elbows,
different kinds of hats worn now
to keep the heat away rather than within.

Only now when the world is alight
and bees buzz and butterflies flutter
and cherry blossoms request smiles,
only now do I see that my mind is a mirror,
a mirror reflecting the light offered by the world
and these new fresh months offer enough light
to fill up the universe.

the page

have you ever written words just
          to feel something
just to heal from something.
          just to peel something back
the layers of an onion resist before they crack.

that first sentence
                    the hardest one to write
words begin to flow in ink as black as
                              night.

emotions pour.
flooding the page 'til it's dripping wet
the page is soaked
                with all these things you left
                              unsaid.

before you sat to write did you even know
                you were upset?
the page is ruined.
                A reflection of your mess.
and yet
                your mind feels softer
because you allowed your emotions
                to leave your head.

Colloquial Headrush

Accent. Your accent.
like oil on skin. Smooth, perfect,
sensual.

Any word.
       All of the words.
            Everything
is perfect
in that accent.
Your accent.

No uncertain words.
No hesitant syllables.

Just this consistent breathwork.
The in and out of reassurance.
The waves of sound
crashing the beaches

      of affection.

Umbrella

Fingers wrinkled, shrivelled by a thirsty ocean
Skin that smells like sunshine.
A girl, her footprints like question marks in sand.
A dog, with helicopter breath.
A man, with no excuse for that sunburn.

No one seems to notice the beauty
of a thousand eyes squinting in the light.
Nor do they appreciate the satisfaction of falling
asleep accidentally beneath umbrellas imitating Atlas.

Their arms stretching wide to block the sun
their backs sacrificed, no complaints.

Tinder

Every 12 hours
I come back here
to see if I
can distil
the potential for love
from photographs.

Daragh Fleming

Special Act

Silently
you showed up
unannounced.
A surprise act in the festival of this life.

Unexpected things
have always been the most
life-changing,
haven't they?

I wish I could say it was always good.
Or maybe not.

For if it was always good
then it would never be good at all.

Accept the things...

You cannot change. When my father first told me
the mantra we were driving the country roads toward
home. I'm not sure if it was light or dark or somewhere in between. I remember feeling young. My
eyes still had the glisten of Spring in them. I never
thought to ask where he had learned it from. I only
knew that it came from him and so must hold some
truth because he was my dad and he knew about
everything. We continued down the road in silence,
patches of green taking up the middle, me turning
over a newfound wisdom, my dad probably recalling
a time when he was broken.

the modern way

I wanted to call and tell you
that I think you're lovely.
But we don't do things like
that these days.

So I liked something you posted on the internet
instead.

Grey Tracksuit

I remember you were here before you left. Gentle as a mist but I could feel you. I don't think anything spells affection like comfortable silences in the car, or taking my hand in yours while we wait for the world to catch up. Tangled in grey tracksuit and you, that night we barely slept at all.

Transcription

I'm sure you know that there are some brands of pain
that are indescribable with words. That is to say –
totally indescribable – for we only have words with
which to describe things.

Difficult pain, complex pain, pain that is soul deep,
beyond the flesh. Pain that we feel no one else will
understand. Like trying to describe a certain scent –
where to even begin?

I think our lives are spent trying to transcribe this
pain. Every moment a word, every experience some
sort of shrouded metaphor. Our whole lives are a
single painting, brushstrokes in attempt to capture
the essence of our personal affliction.

So that at the end we can look back upon this canvas
and slip away. Knowing we gave it everything, show-
ing the world what it all meant.

[Pa]t[i]e[n]c e

Clocks are full of noiseless sound
The silence of seconds passing
is the sound at the end of [life].

I once told you that dying does not scare
me, but being [without] life does. It was
a Tuesday, the air either damp or cold.

People treat the dentist's and funerals the same,
don't they? One day will be the last appointment
No [love] shown to lifeless teeth. Hair done up
all proper but not the way you'd always worn it.

[Is] it really so simple? The answer.
 Just be patient.
Things always work out in the end.

The end.

A thing we all face but rarely acknowledge.
[Death] is the end,
but is the end death?

Morning Prayer

I walk to the end of the lane
and breathe in the dawn.
My chest rises with the sun.
Its life blazing red
behind shut eyelids.
I hear the birds waking
one another up,
sending prayers into the new sky
and I send one too
and open up my eyes
to leave the sun kiss
the only part of me to consent.
My chest falls again.
The breath seeps out to join the clouds
and now, knowing our prayers are received,
The birds and I,
begin.

Acknowledgements

Writing, as a process, happens in isolation, but it doesn't come to be in a vacuum. There are so many factors that influence the work, and allow it to become what it needs to become. A huge thank you is due to Rebecca Rijsdijk who has published my work before and encouraged me to send her a manuscript. Her insight and deep understanding has made this collection the best version of itself, and she is a true champion of poetry.

Friends like Faye Proctor, Adam Shove, Galia Admoni, Lucy Holme, Patrick Holloway, Lousie Nealon (the list is infinite) have been thoroughly encouraging and helpfully critical, allowing the work to grow and take up the necessary space.

Thank you's needs to be reserved for the writing community of Ireland, as well as the Arts Council of Ireland, West Cork Literary Festival and Books Ireland Magazine, writing.ie, and the Irish Writers Centre. These groups and many more have been incredibly welcoming and supportive throughout the years. I've always said encouragement can be the difference between giving up and enduring, so encouragement from all of the people I've crossed paths with is appreciated beyond words.

To friends, family members, and internet users, who've received unsolicited versions of some of these poems to read and give feedback on - thank you. Knowing that readers find value in the work is important, and the best feeling I get through poetry is knowing that I've touched on something that personally affects the reader.

I am quite certain that I haven't thanked everyone here. There are so many people who have made the work possible. A litany of literary magazines who have championed my work, a multitude of writers I deeply admire who've told me to keep going when I've needed it most. My dog Lexi, who gets a mention in the work and doesn't care at all about how successful or unsuccessful I am, the people who support my work but don't read because they aren't readers, those who read the blog, those who watch the videos - anyone who just wants to see others doing well. A thank you is due to each and every one of you, too.

About the Poet

Daragh Fleming is an author and poet from Ireland. Daragh explores themes of existentialism and meaning using a conversational style, and his work has been published widely. You can find more of his writing and poetry on his website, thoughtstoobig.ie. Connect with him on social media for updates and more insights on life and poetry: Twitter (@daraghfleming), Instagram (@daraghfleming), and TikTok (@thoughtstoobig).

Other books by Daragh
'Lonely Boy' published by BookHub Publishing, 2022
'Poems That Were Written On Trains But Weren't Written About Trains' published by Dark Thirty Poetry, 2022
'If You're Reading This Then Drink Water' published by Riversong Books, 2019

Previously Published Works

'Double Exposure' was first published by Cork County Council, 2022
'Damp Skull' was first published in the Fear-Less Poetry Anthology, 2022
'I Wish' was first published by Eat the Storms

About the Publisher

Sunday Mornings at the River is a poetry publisher that is dedicated to elevating and amplifying the voices of poets who are often marginalized or overlooked by the traditional publishing world.

At Sunday Mornings at the River, we are committed to creating a thriving literary community that is based on healthy and inclusive collaborations. We believe that everyone has the right to be heard, and we strive to provide a platform for poets to share their work with a wider audience.

Our focus is on publishing poetry that is thought-provoking, challenging, and that speaks to the unnamable aspects of the human experience. We believe that poets have the power to name the frauds, take sides, start arguments, and shape the world, and we are always on the lookout for new voices that are pushing the boundaries of traditional poetry.

As an independent publisher, we are dedicated to promoting equality and inclusivity in all of our endeavours. Whether we are working with established authors or helping emerging poets to get their work out into the world, we are committed to creating a welcoming and supportive environment for poets of all backgrounds and experien

Scan me
for more books
by Sunday Mornings
at the River

w: sundaymorningsattheriver.com
e: hello@sundaymorningsattheriver.com
ig: @sundaymorningsattheriver